Lightworker Archetypes

Honoring Our Sensitivities
& Remembering Our Gifts

LIA RUSS & MEGHMA HIRA

Lightworker Archetypes

Honoring Our Sensitivities
& Remembering Our Gifts

SILVER PATH
PUBLISHING

For additional material related to this book, visit *www.light workerslifeline.com*.

This book contains references to websites, which were current as of December 2022 but may change in the future.

The Archetypes we discuss in the book are meant to enhance your understanding of yourself and the spiritual world. Think of them as spiritual tools. We do not represent that all of these methods will work for everyone. Therefore, we caution anyone from using them without supervision in any kind of dangerous situation. Always prioritize your physical, emotional, and mental safety.

Cover illustration and book design by Meghma Hira @ego.alchemist. Final typesetting by David J. Perry.

Body text set in Literata and Source Sans Pro, with headings in Vintage Moon and Dreaming Outloud.

Paperback edition   ISBN 979-8-9877045-0-9
E-book edition   ISBN 979-8-9877045-1-6

Contents

Acknowledgments

First, we would like to thank the Universe for bringing Meghma and Lia together. It was one of those meetings that so easily could have ended up in two ships passing in the night, without ever connecting. The fact that our gifts are so perfectly suited to each other, that the Universe had been asking more of each of us than we were prepared to bring to fruition by ourselves has created a magical synergy and a friendship that we will be eternally grateful for.

We would also like to thank David Perry for his editing and publishing advice. His vast knowledge and infinite kindness and patience have been such a help to two neurodivergent, non-linear thinkers!

We would like to thank all the Lightworkers who have come before us, paving the way for centuries in almost total darkness, so that our way would be easier. We would like to acknowledge all the work of the old souls who return over and over again to this planet to help shift the consciousness of us all. And most of all we thank the Creator, the Source, for the unity, love and magic that flow around and through us constantly, even when we close our senses that perceive such things, believing we are alone or abandoned.

Preface

This book came about from a desire to shed light on what it can look and feel like to have gifts, to use them, and not be aware of them — or the opposite, what it looks like to have a gift that you are not using. What most people do not realize is the *tremendous impact* that either of these situations can have on our ability to feel good in our skin, our state of mind, and our immune system. We describe these possible effects for each archetype in the book.

Initially we created an assessment quiz that analyzes your answers and tells you, in percentage terms, the gifts you have worked with (either consciously or unconsciously) throughout your life.

As we explored each of these gifts and wrote about them, this book came into being, and we are very excited to share it with you!

If you haven't taken our Archetype Assessment Quiz yet, you can find your Lightworker Archetype at this link:

https://lightworkerslifeline.com/
home/archetype_assessment/

For more about the mission of Lightworkers Lifeline, see page 103.

Introduction

Identifying Your Gifts

Have you ever wondered what your gifts are? Or how to safely access and develop them? Have you been told that you are a healer or energy worker but don't have the slightest idea about moving forward?

Sometimes our gifts are not so easy to identify. This is partly because we are immersed in cultures that fear, wish to control, or do not understand them.

Although many of us wish that Hogwarts existed, the reality is most of us do not have teachers to guide us in navigating our multidimensionality (see page 4 for the meaning of this term) and our spiritual gifts. While all the gifts discussed in this book can be divined and developed on our own, it is much easier with guidance.

Exploring your psychic gifts alone can be confusing and scary. Having a seasoned guide to validate your experiences allows you to progress in leaps and bounds with confidence.

Introduction

Ten Archetypes

In the following pages, you will get to know the ten Light-worker Archetypes that we have explored.

Each Lightworker Archetype is accompanied by a detailed description along with:

- A bulleted quick reference summary of the Archetype

- A "Power Move" exercise designed specifically to protect or empower the Archetype

- Crystals and stones to enhance the gifts of the Archetype

- In-depth discussion of the Archetype, including possible pitfalls and challenges

- Training or study recommendations

Introduction

Expanding your consciousness is not always comfortable!

As you explore the topics in this book more deeply, please keep an open mind. You may encounter things that seem outrageous to you. This is to be expected. We are beginning a paradigm shift, and those can be fraught with things which are not comfortable — because of their foreignness in the old paradigm.

Change is inevitable. New discoveries in science are turning old ideas (long cherished by some) on their heads. For instance, scientists have discovered cognizance in single celled slime molds and found that pigeons are able to identify old masters' paintings better than college students. All these things and more point to a need to change the way we look at the world, and not just scientifically.

Everyone has different gifts. Some people have experienced healing others; some have been aware of leaving their bodies and being shown things that later are revealed as true. No one knows everything about these gifts, and there is a shortage of information because so many elders and written teachings were destroyed by political and religious institutions over thousands of years.

The quantum field

At the subatomic level, everything in our universe exists in the form of mysterious entities or fluid-like substances called quantum particles that interact with each other via force fields.

These quantum particles defy the laws of classical physics and have been observed to respond to conscious thoughts. They also behave as waves of frequency, much like light energy.

At the most granular level, we (and everything around us) are all swirling and bouncing light particles dis-integrating and reintegrating spontaneously inside a huge force field that connects everything together. This is the true nature of our physical reality.

The multidimensions

The world we experience through our physical bodies is a three-dimensional space. This is the reality that our physical senses report back to us.

However, there are many layers of existence in the universe that aren't perceivable to the five corporeal senses. These energetic dimensions often exist together, overlapping but never interfering with one another. Some of them hold records and information of all events that ever occurred in the quantum realm (past, present, and future), while other dimensions are the homes of our angels, cherubs, dragons, and spirit guides.

Only recently, humanity is beginning to realize that our DNA has a multidimensional nature, containing the codes to access information from space-time dimensions beyond ours. We can facilitate this by opening up to the innate abilities of our bodies and tapping into the frequencies of these dimensions.

For more definitions of terms used in this book, see the Glossary on our website, https://lightworkerslifeline.com/home/glossary/

Humans are able to be aware of, interpret, generate or move energy through various systems within the body. These abilities include:

- **Clairvoyance**, the ability to visually perceive spiritual energies, such as seeing spirits or getting messages in the form of visions.

- **Clairsentience**, the ability to feel spiritual energies as emotions and or sensations, such as experiencing the sentiments of other humans or animals.

- **Clairaudience**, the ability to hear spiritual energies in the form of disembodied voices, high-pitched frequencies, or ringing in the ears.

- **Claircognizance**, the ability to have information suddenly appear in your mind as though downloaded from an outside source into your head.

- **Clairolfactance** or **Clairalience**, the ability to sense spiritual energies as scents, such as smelling the cologne of a loved one who has crossed over.

Throughout this book, we will use the term 'clairs' to denote all the gifts that begin with *clair* — clairvoyance, clairsentience, etc.

Lightworker Archetype

TELEPATH

**Honor Your Sensitivities
& Remember Your Gifts**

Telepath

(Psychic, Intuitive)

Telepaths often:

- Perceive thoughts that aren't their own
- Recognize themes in the collective thought consciousness
- Communicate non-verbally
- Transfer thought energy through the pineal center
- Experience brain fog or migraines
- Are overwhelmed or anxious in crowded places

Power Move for Telepaths:
Meditative Observation

Recommended Stones or Crystals:
Ulexite, White Topaz, Tektite, Blue Calcite and Cavansite

Telepath

Knowing when someone is thinking of you from a distance, spontaneously finishing sentences of those around you, or humming a song that your friend was thinking about are examples of telepathic communication.

Telepathy or thought transference is the most commonly known and accepted psychic phenomenon. Telepaths interact with the energy of thoughts through their pineal center (or third-eye chakra) and can exchange information with others. This transference of energetic data can take place either voluntarily or involuntarily.

If Telepaths intercept thoughts from around them without being aware of doing so, this can lead to anxiety, confusion, and false information because they will automatically assume this is occurring individually

to them. In this case, they will look to their life events to find the source.

But if they were aware the thoughts originated in someone else, they would react differently.

Not being aware of the source makes validating what they are receiving much harder, and so Telepaths, without guidance, can feel overwhelmed, hate their gift, or even convince themselves that they are crazy.

Telepaths can intercept thoughts broadcasting from those close to them (or at a great distance) in the form of ideas or visions. This depends upon whether the Telepath is dominantly claircognizant or clairvoyant.

If you think about telepathy as an open tube, reaching from one person's energy field into another's, you may realize that there are two ends to this tube. This indicates that the energy or thoughts could run in both directions. There is the possibility of Telepaths affecting others' thoughts without realizing it. This is a good reason to get your gift to a place where you can feel when you are using it and consciously control the direction of the flow.

We do not recommend using any of our gifts to cause others to act out of alignment with their free will. You will find that the more integrity you conduct yourself with, the more you are in alignment with the Source (God, the Creator, the Creative Source of All). Our new evolution is to recognize our own divinity and align with that.

Acting in selfish, manipulative ways will lower your vibration, possibly trapping you in a lower vibrational dimension. The choice, as always, is yours.

Telepaths can also receive information from the collective consciousness. This can allow the Telepath to be privy to events happening on the other side of the planet before they are broadcast on the worldwide news.

It can be overwhelming for Telepaths to be in a crowded place as their brains can get overloaded with the thought energies of other people or entities. After a long day with friends or at the workplace, telepaths can benefit from being alone to rest their highly receptive minds.

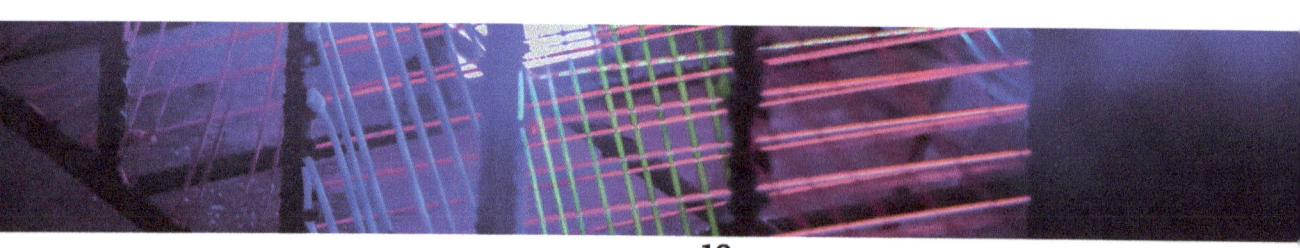

Telepath

Meditative Observation

Having a meditative mind can allow Telepaths to tap into their gifts without being overwhelmed or confused. We are not talking about a specific type of meditation, but simply utilizing whatever practice brings you peace, feeds your soul, calms you and grounds you. Practicing meditation regularly can help Telepaths develop the lens of a calm observer and filter information from the thoughts passing through their highly receptive brains.

Telepath

Needs No Words to Know What's Up

A Telepath would benefit from taking a **Psychic Development** class to practice working with the different clairs and understand them somatically. It is important to understand that, when using the energetic receiving, processing and sending centers located in our bodies, the feedback they give us regarding all these procedures is sensory. So to master any of these skills, we need to master this sensory language. Without bodily awareness, it is more difficult to isolate and work with our clairs.

Notes

Lightworker Archetype

EMPATH

Honor Your Sensitivities
& Remember Your Gifts

Empath

Empaths are often:

- Perceptive of another individual's feelings or intentions
- Nurturing individuals who have open Heart Centers
- Sensitive to emotional energies
- Able to register energies on the surface of their skin (i.e., tingling sensations)
- Apt to experience mood swings and/or heightened emotions
- Susceptible to self-neglect and people-pleasing

Power Move for Empaths:

Conscious Boundaries

Recommended Stones or Crystals:

Aragonite Star Cluster, Green Amethyst (Prasiolite) and Infinite

Empath

Empathy is the ability to perceive another individual's mental or emotional state. Empaths are adept at reading energy, whether they do it consciously or not. Whether Empaths are born or are created by need remains to be determined. However they come to be, they are hyper-aware of others' moods.

Growing up, Empaths may have been the ones comforting the adults in the house, helping them regulate their emotional pain and dysfunction. This can trap the Empath into a chronic habit of self-neglect for the sake of taking care of others.

Until they learn how to erect energetic boundaries (and permit themselves to use them), Empaths are wide open to the emotional states of those around them.

Becoming familiar with his or her gift and recognizing how it feels when activated will help the Empath.

It is extremely important to learn to differentiate emotions that come from outside oneself as opposed to those that come from within.

An Empath can often be more aware of how someone else is feeling than that person may want to admit.

Being with someone who is narcissistic, passive-aggressive, in denial, or lying can wreak havoc on an Empath.

People with the gift of empathy are heart-centered and nurturing individuals who form deep relationships with others.

Empaths largely operate through their heart chakra (the spiritual portal of compassion) and strive to pour love into a world that has only taught them pain.

Living through many hurtful betrayals and fallouts, as often happens, doesn't dim the light of true Empaths.

Empaths have the underrated gift of clairsentience; they are often able to read energies through their skin and feel the energy of their environment in their bodies. If you feel tingling sensations on your skin as energies shift around you or when you walk into a room, you might be a powerful Empath!

Empathic people also may have a deep connection with their sacral chakras (the spiritual portal of sensations and connection), which enables them to connect with other humans in ways that are rare and priceless.

Unregulated emotional energies and lack of discernment around the information they are picking up from others can lead Empaths to experience extreme mood swings and heightened emotions. They often get labeled as "too sensitive" and treated as an inconvenience by the current mechanistic society.

It is highly important for Empaths to have friends who practice integrity and are congruous in their commitment to truth.

Empath

🐾 Power Move for Empaths 🐾

Conscious Boundaries

Imagine the toll it takes on an Empath to feel, in real time, everything that others around them are feeling. Having clear awareness of their own limits in dealing with the emotional energies of others and setting guilt-free boundaries of their own can help Empaths avoid a lot of pain and exhaustion.

Empath

Feels the Truth Beyond What Is Expressed

Training Recommendation

Empaths may be drained because they are not shielding themselves properly or they have accepted others' energies as their own. Meeting with other Empaths who have already made strides in dealing with these energies and creating boundaries can be very helpful. Also taking a basic class in **Grounding and Shielding** as well as **Energetic Hygiene** is recommended.

Notes

Lightworker Archetype

SEER

Honor Your Sensitivities
& Remember Your Gifts

Seer

Seers often:

- See into another's energetic truth and possible outcomes
- Access quantum information through the pineal center
- Are visionaries with a pronounced gift of clairvoyance
- Have vivid and prophetic dreams (or visions)
- See into future timelines
- Suffer from blurry vision, headaches, or exhaustion

Power Move for Seers:

Validation Journaling

Recommended Stones or Crystals:

Ulexite, White Topaz, Tektite, Blue Calcite and Cavansite

Seer

Seers are visionaries and oracles. They can receive accurate information about future events. This may happen once, or repeatedly during their lives.

Like Telepaths, Seers have an active pineal gland or third-eye chakra. But Seers primarily gather information from the quantum field rather than the minds of other humans. They travel through their pineal center to visit other places and bring back information that isn't accessible to linear minds.

Although Seers are predominantly clairvoyant, they can experience "seeing" with other clairs. For example, Seers who are clairaudient receive information as if hearing it spoken.

Sometimes the information that Seers receive, because it comes from a nonlinear origin, can be hard to translate and therefore difficult to validate. For example, you are driving and all of a sudden you receive a picture of a deer standing in the road ahead of you. How far ahead might that deer be? Was it there earlier today (and you are just seeing the energetic residue of its passing) or will the deer be in the road an hour after you pass? These are the questions that can plague Seers.

Even if 50% of the time your visions are validated, the ambiguous nature of these communications can leave you frustrated and confused.

For Seers, perhaps more than any other Lightworkers, spending time tuning into their inner language and comparing the nuances of sensations that accompany each communication is vital if they hope to develop their gift into a useful tool.

As children, Seers may have "suffered" from "overly vivid imaginations." They may have been aware of the extraordinary underneath the mundane. This amazing gift can cause Seers to feel isolated from their friends and family who don't share similar perceptions.

Seers are known to have precognitive visions or dreams. These could be exhausting for the Seer because, if the information is foreign enough, it can take a lot of energy to bridge the gap between "ordinary" experience and the nonlinear information. Consequently, Seers may suffer from migraines or blurry vision when they do not know how to tune their physical bodies to their spiritual gifts.

Though this sounds like a very cool psychic gift, it can be very frightening if Seers do not understand their gifts. They often hide these encounters due to fear of being labeled as out of their minds, or even being stoned or burned at the stake (as happened in earlier times).

Seers are called so for their ability to see into future timelines. But their predictive wisdom can get Seers blamed for causing an unfavorable event when all they tried to do was warn people and prepare them for it.

Seers who also have the gift of clairsentience and/or claircognizance can excel in the art of divination. They are able to read the symbology of the tarot or oracle cards as jumping-off points to retrieve specific answers from the quantum field.

Again, what comes naturally to these amazingly gifted human beings is often feared by society as unnatural or even evil!

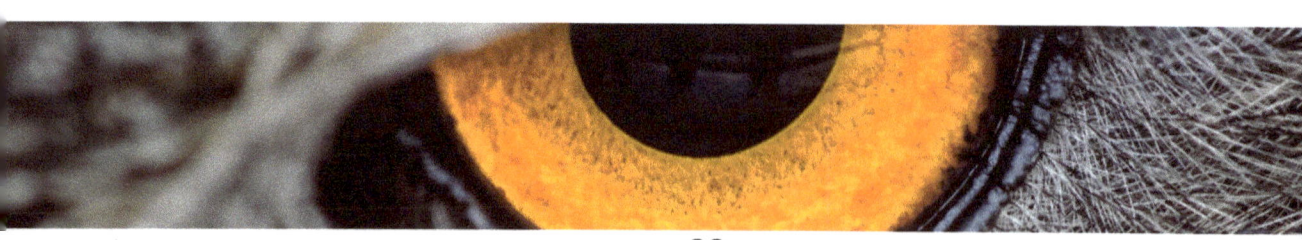

Validation Journaling

Seeing things that others don't can be a very difficult and isolating experience; one may succumb to the fear mentioned earlier. Building the habit of recording all messages that they receive and what transpires afterward will help Seers grow trust and confidence in themselves and their superpowers.

Seer

Knows How Everything Will Play Out

Training Recommendation

The biggest problem Seers can have is a difficulty in establishing a sense of validity for their visions. Setting up situations where you can test your predictive ability and taking notes on the outcomes can help you develop your understanding of the language that your gift communicates with. Using **Tarot** or other such forms of divination can be very helpful in this process.

Notes

Lightworker Archetype

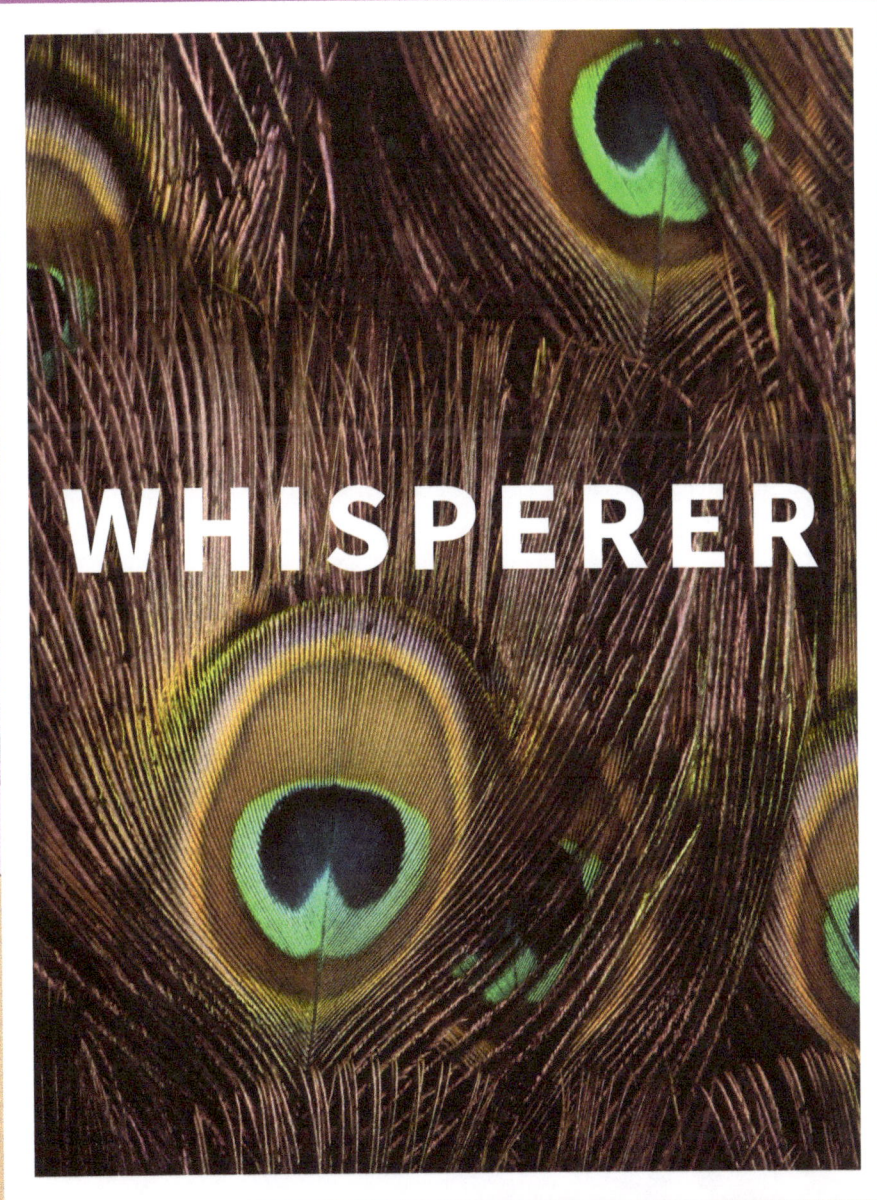

WHISPERER

Honor Your Sensitivities
& Remember Your Gifts

Whisperer

(Animal Communicator)

Whisperers often:

- Work intuitively with the innate wisdom of living bodies

- Are compassionate individuals who make others feel safe

- Understand those who can't communicate their needs verbally

- Experience strong empathy toward the living world

- Are prone to unfulfilling relationships and a need to "fix" people

- Struggle with guilt or shame around their unmet needs

Power Move for Whisperers:

Honoring Your Awarenesses

Recommended Stones or Crystals:

Green Calcite, Pink Calcite, Opaque or Clear Blue Chalcedony and Iolite

Whisperer

Whisperers are the communicators between the innate parts of our being and the mundane world. They are like Mediums for living bodies.

They are able to translate the unspoken needs or feelings of others into verbal language. This ability to understand nonverbal communication places them in a unique position to help those struggling with an inability to communicate in any other way. Often simply being "heard" for the first time can bring significant relief to tortured souls.

Soul Whisperers intuitively read frequencies and energies combined with body language, so they non-verbally understand humans and animals, as well as other life forms. Because of this, they find that they are excellent at working with crystals.

Whisperers have the amazing gift of making others feel safe. This ability functions across species, speaking in the soothing vibration of the most universal language ... LOVE.

Some whispers speak directly to the wounds inside, even in the case of beings that are severely disconnected from their souls. They can even convince separated parts of the soul that it is finally safe to return to the body.

Their simple presence can bring much peace, calm, and serenity to those close to them. This makes them an extraordinary asset in working with people who have post-traumatic stress, depression, or anxiety. Whisperers also can help people open their hearts to the love of Spirit and the wonders of life. Due to their ability to access information from the innate wisdom of another's body,

Whisperers can seem to be intuitive geniuses.

Whisperers, because of their sensitivities, can feel responsible for "fixing" others and can spread themselves thin trying to make others comfortable (due to their empathic abilities). It is important to remind Whisperers to fine tune their abilities to communicate with their own inner reality and work with their needs.

Whisperers can also be very sensitive to rejection or harsh treatment from others and can find it hard to deal with coldhearted people who do not share their ability to love and listen to others.

Because this ability comes so easily to Empaths and Whisperers, they can fail to realize that others may not be able to comfort them in these deep ways. Giving this assistance to others and never (or rarely) receiving it back can be a bitter pill to swallow at first.

This can cause much heartache and soul-searching for Whisperers, because they may falsely believe that not receiving in-depth support in return is their own fault. Rather, they need to seek out other Whisperers or Empaths to receive comfort from.

&❧ Power Move for Whisperers ❧&
Honoring Your Awarenesses

Spend time with something (plant, animal, mineral) and write down what you "hear," feel, or become aware of. Whispers employ many gifts to read energy. They can utilize telepathy, clairaudience, clairvoyance and clairsentience. These gifts can be so enmeshed in their way of sensing and connecting that they may not realize what they are doing. Writing down what you experience with different natural objects or beings can reveal the gifts you are already using. It can also suggest others that you might want to explore.

Whisperer

Soothes Even the Most Tormented Souls

Training Recommendation

Most whisperers have one species that they most readily connect to, and which responds noticeably to them. If you have not experienced this yet, get in the habit of spending time with different animals.

Taking an **Animal Communication Course** would be very helpful for those with this gift, or an interest in developing it.

Notes

Lightworker Archetype

HEALER

**Honor Your Sensitivities
& Remember Your Gifts**

Healer

(Medicine Man / Woman)

Healers are often:

- Able to read and balance the energies of living systems
- Loving individuals with open Heart Centers
- Sensitive to spiritual vibration and touch
- Attractive to humans, animals and spirits in need of help
- Apt to generate heat in their hands when they encounter those who need healing
- Prone to ignore self- care and give too much to others

Power Move for Healers:

Connecting with Nature

Recommended Stones or Crystals:

Vesuvianite, Blue Aragonite, Prehnite and Hiddenite

Healer

The name of this archetype says it all! Healers heal themselves and others who cross paths with them. The world desperately needs such individuals! Ironically, healers can be deeply wounded themselves.

Owing to Healers' beautiful and magnetic energy, people often find them very attractive. Their healing energies are often confused with love interest or sensuality, making Healers subject to unwanted amorous advances.

Healers have wide-open heart centers through which they pour love, compassion, and life into the world. Many have experiences of miraculously healing others or themselves without formal medical training or knowledge.

Wounded people, animals, plants, and even energetic beings in need of healing energy are drawn to them. They can interact with any of these and guide them into recovery.

Like an Empath, Healers can read energy, but not just emotional energies.

With training, a Healer can identify sluggish or blocked energy and intrusions in the auric field or the body, all of which can cause dis-ease.

Healers often have sensitive hands, due to being attuned to the subtle energy chakras and tunnels (nadis) on their palms and arms. This can be experienced as a tingling sensation or a feeling of heat in these areas.

Noticeable heat in the hands during contact with others is almost always a sign of healing gifts. Trained Healers are often able to sense the energetic blockages just mentioned in the palms of their hands when they hold them over a blocked area on someone's body.

Healers channel Universal Life Force Energy, known as Qi in Chinese medicine. The Qi responds to the benevolent intention of Healers and follows their loving direction to flow into another being and naturally encourage its healing.

Depending on what gifts you have developed so far, your healings may be combined with clairvoyance, you might see peoples' auras, or you might be able to see energy blockages in people. If your gift includes clairsentience, you might intuitively know which areas to check for blockages just by being near someone. If you are also clairaudient, you might hear vibrations that are "off" or you may find that you are alerted by ringing in your ears or other sounds.

We can't stress enough how all of these gifts have the potential to be developed and to work with each other, often surprising us by overlapping beautifully.

Being so concerned with healing and helping others, Healers often neglect their own self-care and healing. They fall victim to self-neglect in order to uphold the image of being a giver or to feel worthy. Healers must prioritize their own health and well-being to maintain a balance between how they give and receive.

Connecting with Nature

Healers can absorb energy from direct or indirect contact with others. Gaia, through her body and all of her extensions (plants, animals, insects, rivers, the directions, the weather, rocks, fairies, nymphs, etc.), is the greatest Healer. By regularly surrendering foreign or toxic energies to Gaia to be transmuted, Healers can receive free and loving assistance from the planet. Having intuitive conversations with plants and wildlife grants Healers subtle medicines to heal themselves and others who cross their paths.

Once we have taken a medicine ourselves, if we are in alignment with this medicine, we become carriers of that medicine, benefiting all we come in contact with.

Healer

Feels the Life Flowing through All Beings

Training Recommendation

Where are you in your relationship with yourself as a Healer? If you are just beginning, we recommend exploring different ways to interact with the body's energies. Taking a class on **Energy Work** (Reiki, chakras, crystals, breath work, smudging, reflexology, acupressure, laying on of hands, flower essences, herbs, etc.) can be a great help in increasing your awareness of energy.

Notes

Lightworker Archetype

MYSTIC

Honor Your Sensitivities & Remember Your Gifts

Mystic

(Mage, Wizard, Alchemist, Sage, Hermit)

Mystics are often:

- Seeking to unlock the mysteries of the Gaian Consciousness
- Spiritual scientists exploring the natural world
- Drawn to the elements of Nature
- Drawn to animism, paganism or other earth-centered belief systems
- Excited by ancient mysteries and esoteric wisdom
- Prone to a remarkable proclivity for solitude

Power Move for Mystics:

Knowing Your Inner Guides

Recommended Stones or Crystals:

Wulfenite, Orichalcum, Cathedral Quartz, Chlorite Phantom Crystals and Goethite

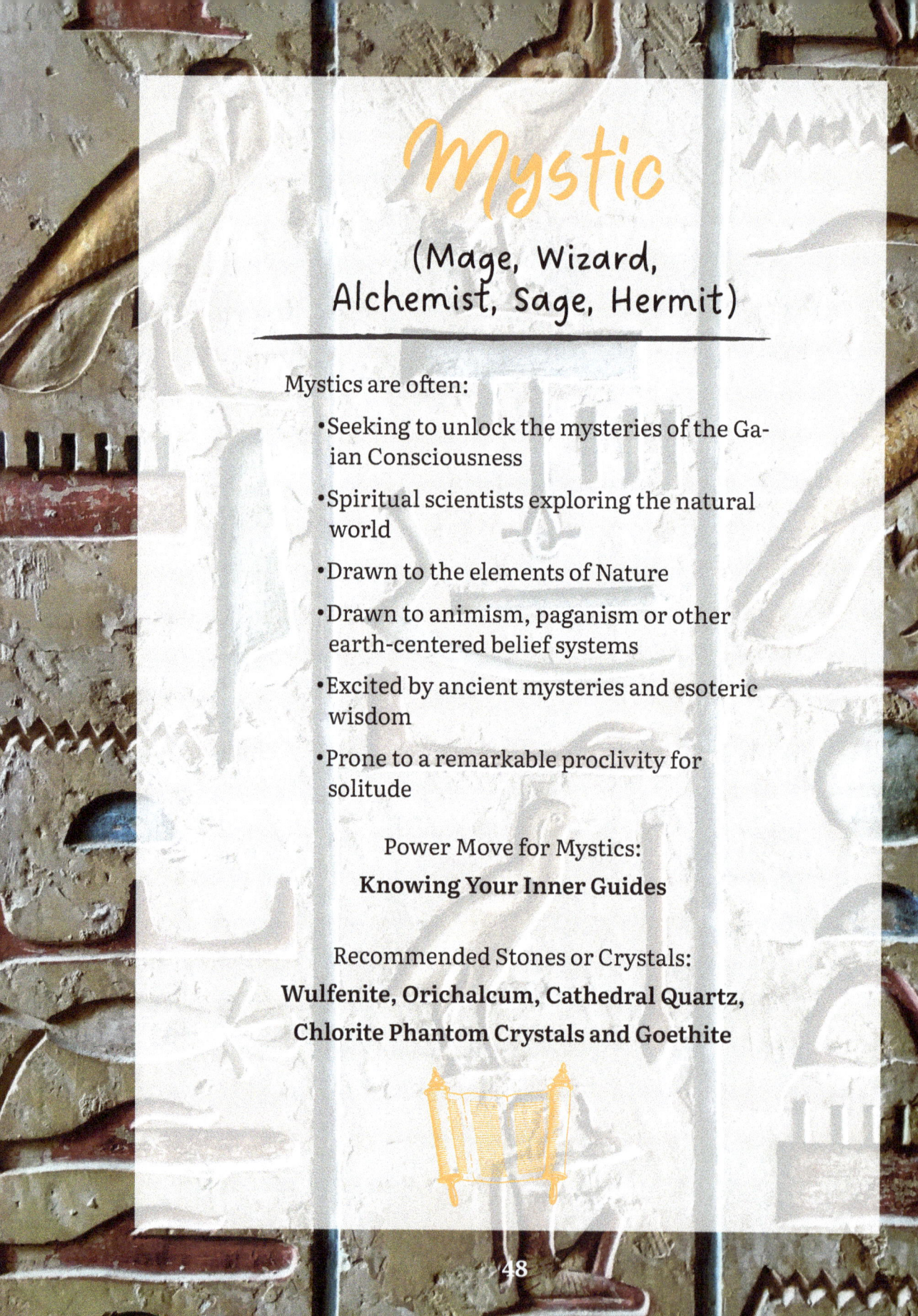

Mystic

Born with an innate connection to the natural world, Mystics need to be in nature as much as or more than with other humans.

Mystics draw energy from natural objects and cannot help but collect them. A young Mystic will bring home all manner of Gaia's creations, from pebbles to shells to bark or moss and even bones, feathers, hair or skins. Mystics are able to feel the sacredness in all of creation and they can spend endless hours watching storms, water, wind or fire.

The Earth and each of these things speak to them (whether they are conscious of it or not) and often reveal the answers to mysteries that elude even scholars.

Due to their (often) insatiable need to obtain esoteric knowledge and mastery, Mystics may go on lifelong quests to uncover the mysteries of nature or life.

Mystics are often the first ones to learn to control the elements, finding that they can increase rainfall or thunder and lightning during a storm.

Those with this gift often do not have physical teachers, but if they can learn to trust themselves, will realize that they have been taught much through their connections to nature, elemental spirits, and Gaia.

Mystics tend to be loners. Their passion for truth and understanding of life makes it hard for them to exist with beings that do not revere the pursuit of such things. Also described as Animists by scholars, Mystics believe that everything in creation has a spiritual essence and that we can communicate with this essence. This puts them in alignment with the belief systems of First Nation peoples, Pagans, Celtics, Druids and Witches.

ᱬ Power Move for Mystics ᱬ
Knowing Your Inner Guides

Mystics are very likely old souls who have carried forward knowledge from past lives. Their connection to their guides is more intact than most peoples' (even if they do not realize it). Mystics benefit from any activity that confirms or validates the accuracy of their inner awareness in the outer world. With practice, they can learn to heed their inner wisdom and guidance to heal themselves, uncover mysteries, obtain new medicines and help Gaia.

Spend conscious time connecting on deep levels to the earth and her creatures. Be open to any form of contact as a direct communication to and for you. Seek out the meaning of these communications and create your own dictionary!

Keep a journal of these interactions and the meaning you draw from them. If you are feeling isolated and alone, look to Gaia as a best friend and allow her to support you and hold you.

Feel through your heart. Believe what you feel and study.

Mystic

Dissolves Illusions to Uncover Truths

Training Recommendation

Mystics have an insatiable thirst for knowledge and they are always in search of higher truths. With all the information available at our fingertips today, it can be difficult to choose a worthwhile rabbit hole to explore. Taking a class on the **Ancient (Egyptian) Mysteries** or **Spiritual Alchemy** can be a great jump start for a Mystic's intellectual and metaphysical pursuits.

Lightworker Archetype

MEDIUM

Honor Your Sensitivities & Remember Your Gifts

Medium

(Channel, Interpreter)

Mediums are often:

- Able to communicate with the spirit realm and other dimensions
- Strong intuitives with non-linear minds
- Channelers with spiritual foresight and active clairs
- Capable of downloading higher knowledge
- Naturally drawn to divination tools
- Conflicted between self-isolation and loneliness

Power Move for Mediums:
Communicating with Higher Self

Recommended Stones or Crystals:
Stellar Beam Calcite, Merkabite Calcite, Cathedral Quartz and Hemimorphite

Medium

Mediums (also known as channels) are strong intuitives with non-linear minds. They often perceive and follow information streams outside their time-space continuum. It's as if they have an internal radar that picks up activities in the quantum field, giving them access to multidimensional guidance and wisdom.

Mediums are the communicators between the spirit realm and the mortal world. They collect messages and guidance from the other side of the veil and pass them on to those in this world.

People who are able to channel information or be a conduit for unembodied spirits can accomplish this via several gifts.

They may hear spoken words or even whole conversations. This would be combining Clairaudience with the gift of channeling.

Mediums may see pictures in their minds, either still single shots (like a photo) or a movie clip. Often these will keep repeating until the medium shares the image(s) with the intended recipient. This is channeling with Clairvoyance.

In addition to Clairaudience or Clairvoyance, a medium may use Claircognizance. This strong sense of knowing can be confusing at first. Without the developed ability to discern what is being sent to you personally, versus what is being sent for another, untrained channelers can make mistakes.

There are those for whom the senses of the nose speak just as clearly as pictures or words. These channels can receive information as scents (Clairolfactance or Clairalience).

It is very important for Mediums to remember that all the clairs can be felt somatically. This is because the mechanisms we have for reading and working with energy are within our bodies. How else would your body be able to communicate to you if not predominantly through sensation? These sensations will likely vary depending on where in your body they are generated. You may even be able to discern the sensations in specific parts of your body as its energy centers are receiving or generating energy. Paying attention to slight sensations and taking note of what is occurring in your environment, as well as internally, is paramount for not just Mediums, but all energy workers who wish to up their game.

Once Mediums have established this understanding and their trust in the higher wisdom coming through them, they can anchor much spiritual foresight and understanding around the events of their daily life.

When you pick information up through your clairs while interacting with someone else, it can be easy to assume the information you receive is for the other person. You must keep in mind that what you saw, heard or felt might have been for you, especially if the other person does not connect with it. When dealing with unseen forces, the ego needs to be monitored carefully.

Owing to the other-worldly source of their wisdom, channels are often met with disbelief and even ridicule! It is not unusual for blossoming Mediums to ignore or try to shut out their gifts for fear of being ostracized or persecuted.

If you are a Medium, you may find that you can use tools like tarot and oracle cards to facilitate your gifts. These can help you interpret messages from your spirit guides, ancestors, and angels.

Communicating with the Higher Self

Being raised in cultures where the gifts of Mediums are feared, or not validated, has made it harder for Mediums to lean into their gifts. Until they do, they will not be able to channel fully.

Knowing something that people around you do not makes it difficult for Mediums to blindly follow the rest of the world (as we are asked to do). Following instructions and doctrines that do not account for personal truth is tantamount to asking Mediums to turn against themselves. They are destined to obey the voice of their Higher Self and their inner wisdom.

Building a strong relationship with their multi-dimensional aspects and communicating with their Higher Self gives Mediums ways to make better use of their gifts.

Automatic Writing is highly recommended for Mediums. Spend ten minutes a day writing whatever comes into your mind, without censoring it. Censoring can come in the form of self-doubt, negative self-talk, gaslighting, and disbelief.

Sometimes the greater the negative self-talk we experience around a thought, the more likely we need to address it. This is also true for resistance; significant resistance to a thought often indicates its power.

Medium

Gathers Intel from Friends in High Places

Training Recommendation

If you are interested in beginning channeling or mediumship, we recommend taking **Reiki 1** and then advancing to **Reiki 2**.

In Reiki 2 you learn how to work on others and do long-distance healing, as well as travel back or forward in time either to heal or to effect energetic changes. The process of channeling universal healing energy to others in Reiki 2 opens you up as a Medium. Many people find that, after taking this training, they start receiving communication for their clients from loved ones who have crossed.

Leaning into the **Tarot** is also a highly effective way for Mediums to learn about how their gift operates. Working with illustrated cards opens up a whole new language of symbols and synchronicities to communicate with the Spirit World. Communications from the Higher Self or Spirit interact with the complex images on these cards. This allows the human mind to find words for thoughts that are non-linear and therefore not normally accessible to humans. Concepts that are beyond our normal range of understanding can find expression using the Tarot.

Notes

Lightworker Archetype

ASTRAL TRAVELER

Honor Your Sensitivities
& Remember Your Gifts

Astral Traveler

Astral Travelers often:

- Project their consciousness out of the physical body
- Access information by interacting with the astral plane
- Retrieve medicine from multidimensional realities
- See their bodies from a higher perspective
- Are prone to being spaced out and to frequent dissociation
- Find themselves exposed to energetic attacks and ailments

Power Move for Astral Travelers:

Practicing Protection Magic

Recommended Stones or Crystals:

Labradorite, Celestite, Moldavite, lidolite, Willemite, Blue Calcite and Covellite

Astral Traveler

Astral projection (also known as astral travel) describes an out-of-body experience (OBE).* This assumes the existence of a subtle body, called an "astral body," through which consciousness can function separately from the physical body and travel throughout the astral plane.

Astral travel involves going to physical places through non-physical means. We arrive at these places without a physical body (although we can interact energetically with, and can be sensed by, those who are physically present).

Often people will astral travel while sleeping and may not be aware of doing so. For example, in Lia's early 20s she went to her first psychic reader,

hoping to learn about her true love and her possible future. She was not expecting to be told that she traveled at night to black holes in space to rescue entities trapped there! Aside from very often waking up exhausted and feeling like she had not slept, she has had no conscious awareness of this process.

Is it important to know if you astral travel during sleep? If your Higher Self is running this, and the small part of your consciousness that operates in the physical world is not needed, then no. However, if you wake up with intense anxiety or fear, perhaps you should look into the possibility.

Sometimes you will have glimpses of travels that you have taken — like a flashback or déjà vu. Some people experience waking up in the night and trying to get out of bed, only to dis-

*There are two other forms of astral projection that are recognized: near-death experiences (NDE) and lucid dreaming.

cover that they have left their physical bodies.

Some Astral Travelers can leave their corporeal bodies on autopilot while they project their consciousness to another location. They can continue tasks such as driving, having a conversation, or just about anything, while their astral self travels. As you can imagine, this can be very disconcerting.

It is possible to astral travel with absolutely no intention of doing so. If you have a strong connection to a person or place in need of help or if you have told Spirit that you wish to be of service, it is possible to find yourself pulled to this person or location. Sometimes being of aid will mean that you first have to travel someplace else to retrieve "medicine." Once you have retrieved the "medicine," you will bring it where it is needed.

Although Astral Travelers do not have physical bodies, they report being able to feel the energy around them. Such energy can be felt outside the astral body, similar to how static electricity feels on your skin or hair.

Having something invisible touch you (especially while astral traveling) can be unwelcome or frightening. So having strong boundaries and shielding is very important.

Remember not to judge something just because of its newness and the discomfort you might experience because of that. Lean into what you feel. If you feel threatened, bring up your shields (and click your heels together repeating "There is no place like home"). Seriously, visualize yourself in a Superman cape, or surrounded by white light, whatever feels appropriate and powerful to you. If none of those things work, you can always leave.

Also, remember that darkness cannot dim light. The only way anything dark can affect you is if you forget who you are (a divine being of light) and start mainlining (vibrating with) the weapons of the dark, namely fear and self-mistrust.

Ask for help when you need it. We are never alone and benevolent spirits are always around us. You can receive shielding and guidance simply by asking.

While astral traveling, a person can pass through pockets of darkness or pockets of radiant light in the astral plane — and they feel equally powerful. Make sure you know how to shield yourself and realize that you can ask for help.

If you haven't experienced astral travel before, it is important to understand that linear concepts and descriptions of the astral plane will never do it justice; so be open to encountering something that you have not experienced before, without judgment.

Outside of our bodies, the world appears different because the experience we have through our physical bodies is linear in nature and constrained by time and space.

When we are in the astral plane, linear time and space do not exist; we can travel great distances (maybe millions of light years) in a blink. Our linear minds may have trouble with this. So one of the biggest things we have to work on, to be successful at astral traveling, is allowing and accepting both new experiences and the dissolution of long-held beliefs.

If we look at space itself, the medicine that it carries is one of continuous expansion. This is evidenced through Dark Matter and Dark Energy (the advancement of the universe since the Big Bang). We can align our selves with this expansive energy by choosing to open ourselves. The act of opening puts us in alignment with 95% of the energy in our known universe! That's a lot of medicine to incorporate in manifesting the life you want.

❧ Power Move for Astral Travelers ☙

Stepping Up Your Protection Game

Stepping into the unknown realms of the astral world without concrete protective measures can leave you vulnerable to energy attacks and/or demonic interference.

A powerful method of conjuring a protective shield is to go into a creative visualization. Ask your guides, ancestors, Higher Self, God or angels to help armor you. See what gifts appear for you. Practice raising and lowering your shields (or armor). If you don't know how to do this, ask for help.

Additionally, validating your subtle somatosensory a-warenesses will be an ongoing process. You will lean into each somatic sensation and identify how you feel regarding it. Then take note of how events play out and use this information as feedback to understand what you were picking up. Knowledge is power.

Astral Traveler

Voyagers of the Uncharted Multiverse

Training Recommendation

If you are Astral Traveling, or planning to do so, understanding what you may encounter, how to deal with it, and how to protect yourself is very important. Research the subject, gather questions, and then get advice from seasoned travelers. Taking a class on **Astral Projection** that covers these topics is easier if you don't have the time for deep exploration on your own.

Lightworker Archetype

SHAPE SHIFTER

**Honor Your Sensitivities
& Remember Your Gifts**

Shapeshifter

Shapeshifters often:

- Blend their energy to travel with or as another animal
- Project their conscious awareness through the pineal portal
- Intuitively perceive vibrational blueprints of other creatures
- See the world through the lens of their host
- Form connections with animal medicine
- Establish complex relationships with their familiars

Power Move for Shapeshifters:

Building an Energy Signature Repertoire

Recommended Stones or Crystals:

Lepidolite, Tiger's Eye, Black Garnet (Andradite) and Iridescent Tergite

Shapeshifter

Shapeshifting in modern times is different than in the past, when humans would receive training from childhood in this art. Without years of training, the type of shapeshifting that is most easily attainable is that of joining our consciousness to that of another being via our pineal portal. When we do this, we can see through the eyes of the being we are joined with. It can be a view through foreign eyes that is stationary. Or it may include moving, sometimes at great speed.

This joining can occur spontaneously or intentionally. If spontaneously, you would suddenly find yourself looking at the world around you with new eyes, literally. Your perspective would be unusual, perhaps higher (like a birds-eye view), or larger than normal (as if you were a mouse looking at a shoe).

If you are shapeshifting consciously, you can envision an animal that you would like to travel with and start by following the movements of this animal in your mind. If you are doing this with a specific creature, always be respectful. Do not attempt to influence its behavior in any way that might harm it.

Blending your energy closely to that of another being allows you to travel close to the other, almost as if you were riding upon its back, or as though you were a similar creature running, flying, or swimming alongside it.

Whisperers, with their ability to be intimately aware of the vibration of other beings, may find that they can join with others' consciousness almost naturally.

Likewise, shapeshifting could come naturally to Healers who can open themselves very deeply to the frequencies of others.

Shapeshifter

🐾 Power Move for Shapeshifters 🐾

Building an Energy Signature Repertoire

Spend more time in nature watching creatures move through their day. Learn their body language and do your best to lean into what they are experiencing. These connections can be felt in your heart. When you can hold the sense of the creature in your heart, send your awareness into your pineal center and imagine traveling next to this creature. Take notes on what you experience. Repeat this often. If a being ever reacts oddly or in a distressed way when you do this, stop. Perhaps you need help in adjusting your amplitude, or you are too emotionally charged, or you need to re-ground yourself in your heart.

Shapeshifter

Sees from More Than One Point of View

Anything that brings you more into alignment with the creature you wish to become will facilitate your ability to travel as, or with, the animal. The keener your somatic awareness of the other, the greater your ability to integrate its nature into your being. Taking classes that involve **Shamanic Journeying, Creative Visualization, Animal Medicine** and working in the **Imaginal Realm** would all be helpful.

Notes

Lightworker Archetype

SHAMAN

Honor Your Sensitivities
& Remember Your Gifts

Shaman

Shamans often:

- Battle dark energies for the health and well-being of those they help

- Are strong and resilient individuals

- Gravitate to unusual knowledge or energies

- Undergo a death/dismemberment and rebirth (or serious Dark Night of the Soul)

- Grow by virtue of finding their way out of the underworld

- Are tormented and feel unable to fit in or tolerate social norms

Power Move for Shamans:
Following the Path of Direct Revelation

Recommended Power Objects:
Feathers, hides, bones, sticks, leaves, flowers, water, wind (breath), earth, stones or crystal

Shaman

Shamanism is the oldest form of healing on our planet. Interestingly, the first Shamans were women. With their need to protect the unborn and the young, women accumulated knowledge of cures and remedies. They also studied both their children and their societies to understand common afflictions — mental, physical, emotional, and spiritual. They searched to discover correlations among and cures for these ills.

In those early days, just as now, there were individuals who had the ability to access different types of knowledge or energies. This facilitated their ability to be healers.

Shamanism is, and always has been, a path of direct revelation, which makes it a perfect path for us to walk today. Each of us has all the answers we seek inside us, but most people are simply not driven enough to take the time to learn how to access this information. But all people can open themselves to follow the path of direct revelation to better their own lives.

I want to make a distinction here. While anyone can practice tuning into the path of direct revelation, and there are many benefits from doing so, this does not make one what I would refer to as a Traditional Shaman.

Traditional Shamans tend to live outside towns or society, like Hermits. But unlike the Hermit, it is not that they crave isolation; rather, the experiences that create Traditional Shamans leave them altered in ways that do not generally help them fit in or tolerate social norms.

Shaman

Traditional Shamans very rarely choose this life for themselves. Most Shamans are created, like diamonds, by life or a higher force.

There are some common themes in the creation of traditional Shamans. One is that they undergo a death and dismemberment experience (or several). This experience takes them to the underworld for a time. When they are able to re-member themselves and find their way back from this darkness and almost total annihilation, they find that they are altered. Perhaps they have new gifts; certainly, their time in the underworld teaches them how to operate in the invisible realms (whether they are aware of it at the time or not). Also, the willpower it takes to re-member themselves gives them tremendous resiliency and strength.

Some Shamans are intercessors between their communities and the spirit world. Others are the intercessors between the plant kingdom and the human one, bringing back knowledge of healing plants. Others walk emotional realms that would shatter most people and come back with an awareness of how others can attain healing or wisdom. Some Shamans astral travel through different dimensions to find cures. Others are like spiritual gladiators and are well versed in battling dark energies for the health and well-being of those they are helping.

If life has chosen you to walk the traditional path of the Shaman, you will have endured some very dark nights of the soul, and you've found your way back. I am not saying you will feel healed, but you don't have to be healed to bring healing to others if you are a Shaman. It's hard (takes time) to heal from intense trauma. Shamanic Healers are not required to be healed—just to have survived. You will now have powerful medicine to share with others. If you are not yet

aware of what this is, it's OK. All things in their own time.

Shamans make use of a variety of tools or helpers that quite literally come into their lives for this purpose. These are very personal, and there is a powerful relationship between them and the shaman.

To the outside observer these tools or helpers may seem quite odd or totally nondescript, while to the shaman they are wondrously magical and powerful.

Haucas (*wakas*), a word from the Quechua language of the Andes, refers to any kind of stone or crystal that the shaman experiences as powerful and healing. Feathers, hides, bones, sticks, leaves, water, wind (breath), fire and earth are all tools shamans employ. Drums, rattles, and flutes can also be used to support healing, journeying, and transformational work. Experiment and be open.

However, you do not need to be a full-fledged Traditional Shaman to access the path of direct revelation and the benefits of this wisdom.

Following the Path of Direct Revelation

Direct revelation means that you do not need an intercessor (priest, minister, rabbi, teacher) to interpret communication to you from God (the universe, spirit, source, nature, ancestors, Higher Self — however you perceive your Source). It also presupposes that all forms of interaction with the world outside yourself can be looked at as communications.

Wandering is a great way to begin or to deepen your ability to be aware of direct revelation (that is, communications from the Source).

Set aside at least 15 minutes to wander. To select a place to wander, close your eyes and take a couple of deep, slow breaths. Consider different destinations and choose the one that you feel most drawn to. Go to that place and begin to walk.

Become as present as you are able and feel the air on your skin. Breathe in any scents and notice any sounds. Give loving consideration to anything that draws your attention. Perhaps the sun is shining more brightly on the trunk, branches, or leaves of a particular tree. Perhaps one bird is singing more loudly than others, or something else catches your attention. Respond to this as an invitation. Follow it. Spend time with it. Pay attention to inner sensations. These are how we take in and understand (with practice) what is being communicated to us.

Each interaction that you have — a leaf falling, the wind suddenly stirring the leaves, a butterfly or squirrel crossing your path — all are present for you at that moment to share their medicine or a message with you.

You may not understand what the actual message is initially but lean into each encounter and see how it leaves you feeling. At first, do not hesitate to look up traditional meanings of such medicine or the message these things bring. For instance, a butterfly represents metamorphosis, trust, faith, or completion. But for you, it might also represent your grandmother, or something else. After a while, you will have your own vocabulary of meanings to assign to each encounter.

This is the path of direct revelation.

Shaman

Carries a Permanent Visa to the Underworld

For those that simply want to follow the path of direct revelation, finding someone who is leading a Shamanic Journey (live or in a recording) will help you to develop your abilities to trust the way Spirit communicates to you in visions. Learning how to drum or rattle in steady rhythms (like a heartbeat) can help you deepen your own travels into shamanic realms. Creative Visualizations, Imaginal Realm work, and Wandering are all good ways to further your ability to tune into the energies of nature and work with them.

As we discussed, traditional initiates of Shamanism are put through emotional and psycho-spiritual trials before they transform into powerful medicine keepers. These experiences can be intense, leaving Shamans feeling fragmented; it can take tremendous fortitude to bring themselves back together. It can be very helpful to study the Dark Nights of the Soul and Shadow Work to gain an in-depth understanding and acceptance of how this work facilitates our spiritual evolution and empowerment.

Notes

Leaning into the Archetypes

Would it surprise you to know that most of us have more than one gift, even if one is dominant and is the only one you recognize? A combination of gifts can create new gifts or applications of gifts, and therefore, undoubtedly, there are gifts we have not yet identified.

Here are examples of gifts we did not include on the archetype list: Anchors, Space Holders, Batteries, Catalysts, Gate Keepers, Wisdom Keepers, Earth Keepers, Earth Grid Supporters, Doorways, Weavers, Tree Mages, Wild Women, Midwives, Ocean Women, Fire Women, Desert and Mountain Women, Crones, Soul Summoners, and Water Carriers. All are equally important.

Every gift is valuable. Furthermore, in this unprecedented time on planet Earth, new gifts are emerging. This is why it is so important to tune into your body and its sensitive awarenesses. No one holds all the answers. You will need to trace threads that seem important to you both back to their source (within and without you — see descriptions of inner and outer gifts below) and forward to their expression in order for you to begin to make sense of your gifts.

Combining gifts is something that occurs naturally. For example, if you are a Whisper or an Empath, it's easy to move into Shapeshifting because you are already in the habit of focusing on and developing a deep awareness of other beings, which Shapeshifting requires.

Shamans often employ Astral Travel to get medicines from other dimensions. Healers can employ many shamanistic tools to facilitate healing, while Shamans heal using spiritual medicine.

Here is another example of the way gifts can combine. If you fall under any of the first nine archetypes, you might be drawn as well to follow the path of direct revelation, which is the path of the Shaman.

Inner gifts

After putting our list together, we noticed that four of the gifts are what we would describe as inner gifts. These gifts involve heightened senses of intuition, empathy, self-awareness, and therefore an ability to sense other beings' states. Those with inner gifts would be Empaths, Whisperers, Healers, and Shapeshifters.

Outer gifts

Then we noticed that four other archetypes have more to do with a heightened awareness of things outside ourselves; these would be the Seer, Telepath, Medium, and Astral Traveler.

Bridges

Interestingly, this leaves the Mystic (Mage, Alchemist, Wizard, Sage, Hermit). Because it's a path of study, this gift functions as a bridge between the inner and outer gifts. We see Shamanism as falling into this bridging space as well.

Notes

Keeping an Open Mind and Heart

Even though we are multi-dimensional beings, since we experience the world in a linear fashion, we are inclined to put events in boxes or ascribe a linear timeline to them. This is our familiar and comfortable way of exploring ourselves and the world around us.

However, as the consciousness on our planet rises, we are being asked to step out of the old linear paradigm in order to assimilate new types of information.

For centuries, the true nature of human existence has been buried under culture, religious mythologies, misinterpretations and stigma. Now all of this is being revealed in the light, layer after layer. Humanity is waking up, questioning the systems that have kept us in the dark for generations, and realizing that the true potential of human beings surpasses our current imagination.

The paradigm shift is challenging everything that we were taught and uprooting the very core of our belief systems. This creates the perfect conditions to reprogram our subconscious.

We encourage you to break down, or at least move through, the walls that limit your beliefs. Preconceived notions can get in the way of receiving brand-new information. Therefore, it is imperative for each of us to learn to trust ourselves and the higher guidance we receive!

In conclusion, there is much to learn even about what is already known, as well as about things not yet available in mainstream consciousness. It's a very exciting time.

Notes

About the Authors

Lia Russ and Meghma Hira were drawn together across oceans and continents by destiny to help individuals who are beginning to explore the gifts discussed in this book to move into their gifts more quickly, with ease, grace, and loving support.

Lia has studied with elders from many nations. For over four decades she traveled the world seeking to understand what humans are, what we are capable of, and how to eliminate the blocks that hold each of us back from fully shining our light in the world.

She specializes in helping others heal, find peace with those root issues and turn them into powerful allies. If you would like to learn more about Lia and her work, she has written a best-selling book, *Connecting The Dots: Ancient Wisdom, Modern Science*, in which she reveals science-based information about our abilities to read, understand and work with energy. She explores ancient knowledge from around the world about humans' innate abilities. She demonstrates how these abilities are tied to biological systems inside us. These systems allow us to pick up, generate and direct energy. Lia establishes that the information our ancestors deduced regarding the world's mysteries was surprisingly accurate.

Lia is clairvoyant, clairaudient, clair-cognizant, and clairsentient. At the age of nine, she discovered that she could heal others.

Lia is dyslexic. Although her neurodivergence makes it challenging for her to operate in the everyday world, it allows her to perceive non-linear realities. It is natural for her to enter the Akashic Records and use her gifts to retrieve information for her clients.

We feel her presence as loving, nurturing guidance, uplifting us to find our gifts and truths. Lia has been referred to as a Spiritual Godmother. Her warmth and accumulated knowledge, along with her gifts, are a wonderful resource to add to your awakening process.

"Move towards your bliss" —
Meghma Hira @ego.alchemist

Growing up in a culture rich in the spiritual and metaphysical beliefs of the East didn't prevent Meghma from being devoured by the mechanical matrix. Conditioned to be "the golden child" of a middle-class family, she pursued "high-paying and reputable" jobs at software startups.

Realizing she had been lured into the illusion of clawing up the corporate food chain while the system digested her alive came to her at a heavy cost. Now wary of superficial living and shallow ambitions that erode our youth and wit, Meghma hit the "eject button." Quitting her job in December 2021, she decided to test the powers of her mind and the Universal Laws of Energy by aligning herself with her higher calling.

What she has learned in the time that has passed between then and now will change the lives of millions of tormented young Lightworkers living in compelled complacency.

Meghma is a multidimensional woman from India who finds herself deeply grounded in mysticism, magic, and other mysteries of the Universe. This is where she feels most at home.

Although her journey was treacherous, she learned it is worth all the adventures leading to peace within.

The divine intelligence and love that many cultures call God expresses itself, learns and loves through sentient beings such as ourselves. It places everything we need on our path and brings us to those who are in need of our light. Meghma hopes to educate, uplift, and learn from the New Earth collective that is aligning the planet to a higher frequency

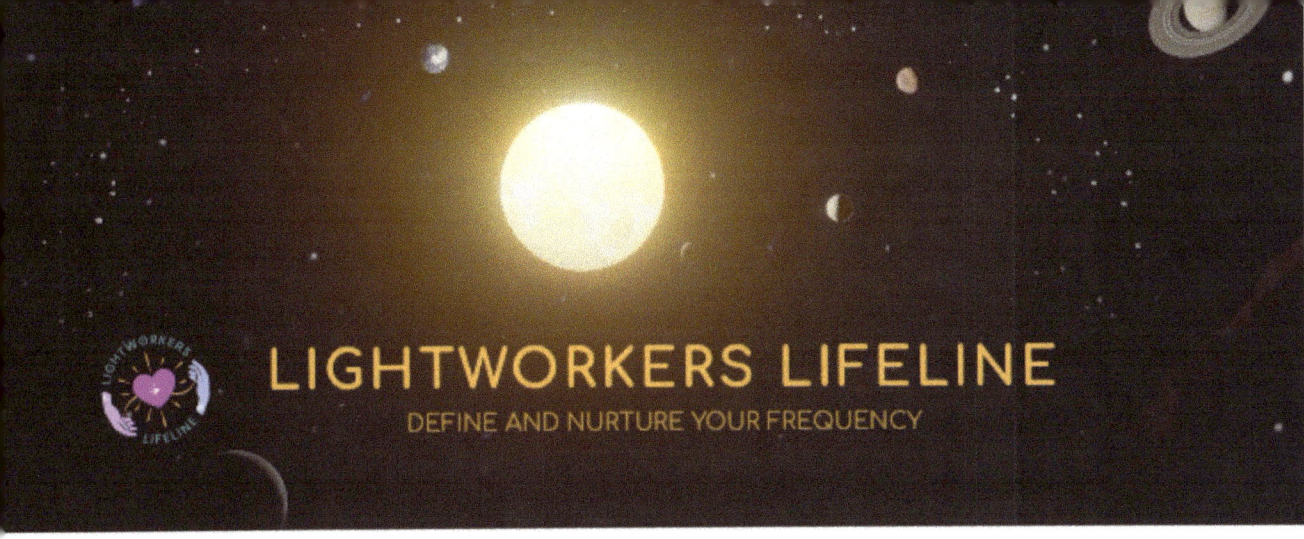

LIGHTWORKERS LIFELINE
DEFINE AND NURTURE YOUR FREQUENCY

Lightworkers Lifeline came about because of a need we recognized in untrained Lightworkers, Healers, Energy Workers, the newly Awakened, those experiencing symptoms of Ascension and Starseeds.

Over and over again, we saw people in need of guidance to discover their gifts, to develop them and work with them, as well as deal with the physical and emotional overloads that these transitions can entail.

We acknowledge that we are all able to access any knowledge that we seek, without teachers or guidance. However, this method is time- and resource-consuming and does not address the questions or insecurities of a novice.

Lia awoke 50 years ago, alone, on a mostly dark planet. She is a perfect testimony that we can figure this stuff out without teachers or guidance in human form. But ask her if she wishes that there had been a Hogwarts or an experienced human she could trust to help her find her truths, and she would reply with a resounding YES!

A vast array of gifts is emerging on earth at this time. Although these gifts are diverse, humans tend to react to them in predictable ways: from betrayal to disbelief, to feeling displaced or dissatisfied with one's current life, work, friends, lovers, etc.

Knowing that you must do something different in your life — but not being able to get clear on what that is — can leave one feeling frustrated and inadequate.

These feelings are to be expected as one is exploring a new paradigm. Comfort with a new reality requires developing new skills and new ways of understanding the universe.

We can help individuals with all of this, and we do so with great joy!

Do You Want To Know What Lightworker Archetype You Are?

We have created an immersive questionnaire to help your answer just that!

Take our free
Lightworker Archetype Assessment

This 10-minute exploration reveals your dominant Lightworker Archetype.
It also identifies how the other archetypes and gifts manifest in your life.

Scan the QR code printed below or visit the following link to get started:

https://lightworkerslifeline.com/
home/archetype_assessment/

Contact Us

 /lightworkerslifeline

@lightworkerslifeline

support@lightworkerslifeline.com

/lightworkerslifeline

www.lightworkerslifeline.com

LIGHTWORKERS LIFELINE
Define & Nurture Your Frequency

Lia Russ & Meghma Hira co-create a powerful incubation portal to help emerging Energy Workers, Healers and Lightworkers **understand and develop their gifts** while navigating the new frequencies on the planet.

Always With You, In Spirit & Love

Photo Credits

The photographs on the first page of each chapter (credited above) are also used as background on the second and third pages. Each chapter has an associated graphic (e.g., the whale on pages 16, 20 and 21). All these graphics were found on Canva, and we would like to thank the artists who made them available.